Amazon Echo Dot User Manual

From Newbie to Expert in One Hour: The Magic of Amazon Echo Dot 2nd Generation

Ray Higgins

All Rights Reserved@ 2017- Ray Higgins

Table of Contents

Introduction

Amazon Echo was a breakthrough in smart technology with the new artificial intelligence called Alexa- which turned it into a game-changing device. Echo made many awesome things possible to control your home, order stuffs on Amazon, listen the news, play music and so on. However, the two main problems were its high price point and its inability to connecting to an external speaker. The **Echo Dot (2ⁿᵈ Generation)**, Amazon's new Alexa output, fixes both of these problems.

The 2ⁿᵈ generation Amazon Echo Dot is a tiny Alexa-powered unit that is cheaper than the Echo and that lets you connect it to an external speaker system with ease. This guide will help you explore the magic of Alexa and get the best out of your Echo Dot (2ⁿᵈ Generation) very quickly.

Setting Up Amazon Echo Dot

In order to get the Echo Dot and Alexa in working order, you need to connect it to a Wi-Fi network, install the Alexa App and register the Echo Dot to your Amazon account. You need to follow these steps:

Step-1: Install the Alexa App and sign in

Alexa App is a free app that can be installed on Android, IOS, Fire devices and computers to manage the functionalities of the Echo Dot. It is compatible with all the latest versions of Android, IOS and Fire OS.

Go to the app store of any mobile device and search for "Amazon Alexa". Then select and download it.

You can also enable Wi-Fi in the computer and go to https://alexa.amazon.com to download the app to your computer.

Please note that Kindle Fire (1st Gen and 2nd Gen), Kindle Fire HD 7 inch (2nd Gen) and Kindle Fire HD 8.9 inch (2nd Gen) tablets do no support the Alexa App as of now.

Step-2: Turn on Echo Dot

You need to place the Echo Dot in a suitable location. Don't keep it too close to a wall or window. Then plug the device into a power outlet using the power adapter. Phone chargers or other similar power adapters may not provide enough power to support Echo Dot.

Once connected to power source, the light on Echo Dot will turn blue and then orange. When the light turns orange, Alexa will welcome you with greetings-

"Hello. Your Amazon Echo Dot is ready for set up. Just follow the instructions in your Alexa App."

Step-3: Connect to a Wi-Fi network

Open the Alexa App in your smart phone. Then follow the instructions in the Alexa App to connect Echo Dot to a Wi-Fi network.

It involves the following:

1) Open the Alexa App from your smartphone. Sign in with your Amazon credentials. Tap on the three horizontal lines on the upper left corner. This will open a navigation panel on the left. Tap on **Settings**.

2) Tap on **Set up a new device**. In the list of devices, you should see your Echo Dot. Tap on it.

3) Next, it will ask you to connect to a Wi-Fi network. Tap on **Connect to Wi-Fi**. Choose your Wi-Fi network and enter your Wi-Fi password, if required.

4) In the next screen, it will tell you to wait for the light on Echo Dot to turn orange. When the light turns orange, click **Continue.**

5) Now it will tell you to go to the Wi-Fi settings of your smartphone and connect directly to the Echo Dot's Wi-Fi connection. The network will be something like "Amazon XXXX". Tap on it. Your phone will connect to Echo Dot. A few seconds later, Alexa will confirm that it is connected to Echo Dot by saying- *"You've connected to Echo Dot. Go ahead and finish the set up in your Alexa App."*

6) On the Alexa App, a **Connected to Echo Dot** screen will appear. Tap **Continue**.

7) Now you need to reconnect to your Wi-Fi network. Tap on your Wi-Fi network from the list. Echo Dot will connect to your Wi-Fi network. The light ring will be orange with a circulating motion. It will take several minutes to synchronize with your Amazon account.

8) When the orange light turns off, it will indicated that the device is ready to be used. The Alexa App will show a notification "Setup Complete". Tap on **Continue** to start using the Alexa App and Echo Dot.

Please note that Echo Dot connects to dual-band Wi-Fi (2.4 GHz / 5 GHz) networks that use the 802.11a / b / g / n standard. Echo Dot does not connect to ad-hoc (or peer-to-peer) networks.

Step-4: Talk to Alexa

Your Echo Dot is now ready to use. "Alexa" is the default wake work. Just say "Alexa" and start speaking naturally and ask questions.

If you want to change the wake word, you can do that from the Alexa app any time. In the Alexa app, go to **Settings** and then select the Echo device and the then select **Wake Word** and change it from the subsequent drop down list. Here are some screenshots of the process:

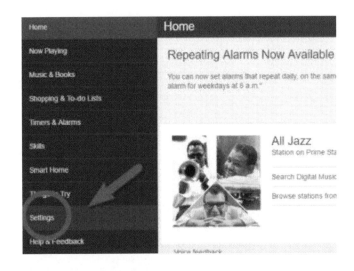

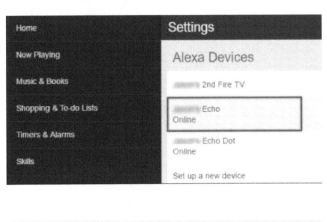

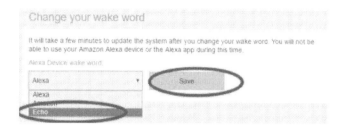

If you want to make sure that Alexa hears your voice, you can enable the wake up sound. From the Alexa App, go to **Settings > [Your Device Name] > Wake Up Sound**. Enabling the wake up sound will mean that the device will produce a beeping sound everytime it wakes up in response to your call.

Now test the device. Say the wake word and listen closely if you hear a soft beep. The beep indicates that the device is fully set up. Ask a few basic questions like:

"Alexa, how's the weather today?"

"Alexa, what's the headline today?"

Alexa should respond to your question and your device is up & running.

How is the 2nd Generation Dot Different from the 1st Generation Dot?

1. The new 2nd Gen Echo Dot is smaller, lighter. It has a glossier finish. It does not have the rotating volume dial. Instead, it has volume up and down buttons.

2. It does not come with the 3.5 mm cable, which was part of the original Echo Dot package.

3. The new Echo Dot is available with a new White Pearl version as well as the usual Black one.

4. It has an improved voice recognition system. A new speech processor has been incorporated to enhance the voice recognition accuracy of the new Echo Dot.

5. Echo Dot 2nd Generation has a new Echo Spatial Perception (ESP) technology. It will be helpful if you have multiple active Alexa devices in your home. In that case, the ESP feature will make sure that when you speak to Alexa, only one device responds instead of multiple responses that would be clumsy.

6. The new Echo Dot has better availability and almost 50% lower price.

Hardware and Basics

Echo Dot is a voice-controlled intelligent device with a small built-in speaker. With 1.3 inch high and 3.3 inch diameter, the Echo Dot is as small as a hockey puck. It weighs 163 grams.

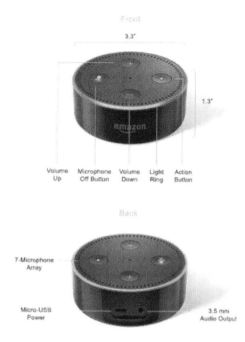

While the software of Echo Dot is similar to its predecessor, the Echo, the hardware is slightly different.

The Dot contains a 3.5 mm audio output jack that can be used to connect to any speaker like the UE Boom 2 or a Bose and turn that speaker into an Alexa enabled device.

You can also prefer to connect the device to your own bluetooth speaker. This small change has made a massive difference since the lack of audio output was a huge complaint with Echo when it first launched.

Configuring for Sound

Connecting to Bluetooth Speakers

The Echo Dot can pair with an external speaker of your choice over Bluetooth. Here is the step by step process of accomplishing that:

Step-1: Make sure that the Echo Dot is connected to a Wi-Fi network.

Step-2: Put the target speaker into pairing mode.

Step-3: Run the Alexa app from your smart phone and go to **Menu > Settings**.

Step-4: Select your Echo Dot device from the list of Alexa devices.

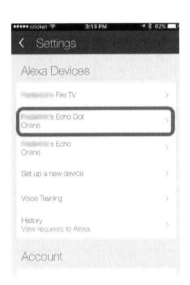

Step-5: Tap **Bluetooth**.

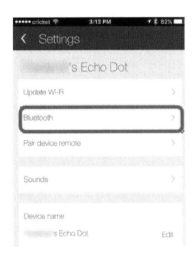

Step-6: You should see your speaker among the list of bluetooth devices. Tap on it. It will complete the pairing in a few seconds.

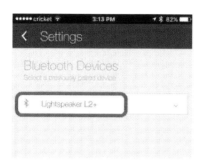

From then onwards, the Echo Dot will route all audio to the speaker whenever the speaker is on.

If you want to remove that speaker, just go to the Bluetooth menu, tap on the speaker and then tap **Forget Device.**

Connecting to External Speakers

You can also connect to any external speaker using a 3.5 mm audio output cable. Just connect the device to the speaker with the cable and the Alexa voice will be carried over to the external speaker.

Playing Music, Podcasts & Audiobooks

One of the main features of Alexa is that you can listen to music from your favorite sites.

Where to play music from?

Well you have a number of choices.

Amazon Prime:

Amazon Prime holds a vast selection of music that you can listen to. It also recommends great music based on the type of music you have listened before.

Spotify:

Spotify is a Swedish site that allows you to listen to songs and albums from the most popular and independent artists around the world. It has over 100 million active users. You can choose from a vast array of music both free and premium.

iHeartRadio:

If you like to listen to old-school radio, iHeartRadio is the platform for you. It has a cool recommender system, music festival, blocking system for music you don't like etc.

Pandora Radio:

It is another music recommendation and streaming service that helps you create a great playlist that suits your taste based on the genre of music you have been listening to. You can rate the songs by applying thumbs up and thumbs down.

TuneIn:

TuneIn has over 4 million podcasts and programs and over 100,000 radio stations that you can listen to. You can also enjoy news, sports, weather and any kind of radio station you want!

How does it Work?

You can ask Alexa to stream audiobooks, live radio, music, podcasts and much more. Alexa services can be made of the streaming services directly. After the Echo Dot has been registered to an Amazon account, the user will have access to all Audible audio books and music that are available in Amazon Music libraries.

The most convenient way to play music is through Amazon Prime Membership. It gives you access to the entire Prime music library. Prime Music library is the default music browsing platform for signed in Prime members.

Upload Your Own Music

Of course, you can upload your own music to the Amazon Music library (www.amazon.com/musiclibrary). Then you can ask Alexa to control the playback and play the music with simple voice commands.

You can also play personal music from Google Play & iTunes with Echo Dot.

You can upload a music collection to Amazon Music library from your PC or Mac using Amazon Music for PC and Mac.

How to Upload Your Own Music from a Computer?

1. From your favorite browser, open your **Amazon Music Library** from the computer where the music is stored.
2. From the left menu, click **Upload Music**. A message might pop up saying that you need to install Amazon Music Importer. Follow the instructions on screen.
3. When the music importer is installed, click on **Start Scan**. This will scan your PC and iTunes library for any music available to be imported. This scanning process can take some time depending on how much music is available. On the other hand, you can also **Browse Manually** if you want to import some specific songs.
4. Once the importer has finished scanning for music available, click on **Import All** to add the whole library. You can select specific music to import, too, by clicking on **Select Music** and choosing the songs that you want to upload.

You can upload up to 250 songs to the music library for free. And if you register to an Amazon Music membership, you can access over 270,000 songs.

Link a Third-Party Music Service to Alexa

You can link your existing account with a music streaming service to Alexa using the Alexa App. You can link third party music services like Spotify, Pandora, iHeartRadio and TuneIn.

Here are the steps involved to link your **Spotify** account:

Step-1: Open the left navigation panel in the Alexa App and tap **Settings > Music & Media**.

Step-2: Tap on "Link account on Spotify.com"

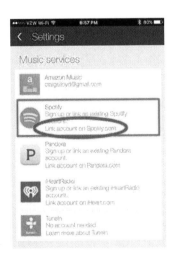

Step-3: Tap on "Log in to Spotify" and enter your Spotify username and password and then tap log in.

Remember that you'll need a Spotify Premium subscription for the Echo Dot integration to work.

How to Listen to Your Music

Simply ask Alexa to play the music and Alexa will do the rest. Alexa will search for the song, album, artist, playlist or genre in your music library and , if not there, it will search the Amazon Prime Music catalog and Amazon Digital Music store.

Some basic music commands are:

Play a specific song >> "Play some music" or "Play the song, '(music title)'"

Play a specific album >> "Play the album, '(album name)'"

Play music by a specific artist >> "Play songs by, '(artist name)'"

Play songs of a specific genre >> "Play some (genre name) music" or "Play some (genre name) music from Prime."

Play a specific playlist >> "Listen to my (playlist name) playlist."

Play Prime Music >> "Play (song/album/artist) from Prime Music" or "Play (playlist name) from Prime Music."

Play Spotify Premium >> "Play (song name) from Spotify." or "Play songs by (artist name) from Spotify." or "Play (genre) from Spotify."

Play a custom station >> "Play my (artist/genre) station on (Pandora/iHeartRadio/Prime Music)."

Play a Radio Station (TuneIn and iHeartRadio) >> "Play (station frequency)" or "Play the station (statin name)"

Play a podcast or program (TuneIn and iHeartRadio) >> "Play the podcast (podcast name)" or "Play the program (program name)"

Skip the next song >> "Skip"

Create a station (iHeartRadio and Pandora) >> "Make a station for (artist name)." or "Create an (iHeartRadio/Pandora) station based on (artist)"

Some common music commands when a music is already running:

Adjust the Echo Dot Volume >> "Volume up/down" or "Set volume to level (number)"

Learn about the details of a running music >> "What is this?" or "Who is this?" or "Who is this artist?"

Stop a music that is currently playing >> "Stop" or "Pause"

Playback Music >> "Play" or "Resume"

Set or cancel a sleep timer >> "Set a sleep timer for (X) minutes/hours." or "Stop playing music in (X) minutes/ (X) hours." or "Cancel sleep timer."

Move to previous or next track >> "Next" , "Previous"

Repeat Songs >> "Repeat"

Like/Dislike a song (Pandora, iHeartRadio & Prime Stations) >> "Thumbs up", "Thumbs down", " I (like/don't like) this song."

If you don't like to hear a song anymore >> "I'm tired of this song."

(**NB**: Some of the above mentioned commands may not work on third party music services like Pandora , iHeartRadio etc.)

Connecting to Other Bluetooth Devices

Connecting to Mobile Bluetooth

1) Go to Alexa App. Tap on the three horizontal lines to go to the left panel and then tap on **Settings**.

2) Tap on your Echo Dot device from the list of devices. Select **Bluetooth > Pair a New Device**. This will set your Echo Dot into pairing mode.

3) Open the Bluetooth settings in your mobile smartphone. You will see your Echo Dot in the list. Tap on it. After a few seconds, Echo Dot will pair with your smartphone. Alexa will confirm the Bluetooth connection with a voice message.

4) You can disconnect your smartphone by simply saying the command, "Alexa, disconnect."

Connecting to a Mobile Hotspot

In order to connect Echo Dot to a mobile hotspot, you need to make sure that the latest software of Echo Dot is installed. Then make sure that the mobile hotspot is on.

1. From the settings menu of your mobile phone, turn on your mobile data. Then turn on the mobile Wi-Fi hotspot. Note the network name and password.

2. Go to the Alexa App, open the left panel and tap on **Settings**.

3. Select your Echo Dot and then tap on **Update Wi-Fi**.

4. Press and hold the **Action** button on the Echo Dot for five seconds. The light ring will turn orange as it tries to connect to your mobile hotspot. Then it will connect with the mobile hotspot.

5. A list of available Wi-Fi networks will appear in the Alexa App. Scroll down and select **Use this device as a Wi-Fi hotspot**. Then tap on **Start**.

6. Enter the mobile hotspot name and password and tap **Connect**. Now Echo Dot will search for your Mobil Wi-Fi hotspot and attempt to connect to it when found. The light ring on Echo Dot will be orange. In a few moments, Echo Dot will connect to the hotspot. Alexa will confirm the connection with a voice message.

Alexa: You Beauty!

With Alexa, there is never a dull moment. The Alexa App allows you to do a lot of things.

Read Whenever and However You Want

Alexa not only works with Kindle, but also work with Audible. So, you can choose whether you want to read a book or listen to it.

Shopping on Amazon

You can shop for various products on Amazon with Alexa. Your Amazon account address and billing information will be the default one set at your Amazon account.

You can tweak settings by asking for confirmation code, see product, order details and even turn purchasing off.

Placing Orders

You can order an item by simply saying, "Alexa, order Towel." Alexa will tell you the item name, price and the estimated order delivery time. The Alexa App will show you the additional details of the product.

You can order Music as well as physical products with voice command. You will need an Amazon Prime membership, a valid payment method and a billing address to get started.

Managing Voice Purchase Settings

1. Open the Alexa App, go to the left navigation panel and tap on **Settings**.
2. Tap on **Voice Purchasing**.
3. You can use the switch to turn on or turn off the voice purchasing.
4. You can add a 4-digit code so that you can confirm your purchase by telling the code.

NB: You need to have **1-Click Purchase** enabled for voice purchasing to work. For that, you need to go to your Amazon.com account and enable your 1-Click payment method.

<u>Some basic commands are:</u>

The Task	The Command
Purchase a Prime-eligible item (up to 12 of any one item)	"Order a [item name]" "Yes / No" (To confirm the order).
Deleting an Item	"Delete [item name]" "Delete Rice"
Reorder an item	"Reorder [item name]." "Yes / No" (To confirm the order).
Add an item to your cart on Amazon	"Add [item name] to my cart."
Cancel an order immediately after placing it	"Cancel my order."

NB: If Alexa is unable to cancel an order, you can cancel it manually from your Amazon account or from the Prime Now App.

Tracking Orders

Alexa can give you an update on your orders on Amazon by telling you the nearest delivery date.

The Task	The Command
Track the status of a recently shipped order	"Where is my stuff?" "Track my order."

Listening to Audiobooks

Audiobooks purchased from Audible and Kindle Unlimited can be played through Alexa. Whispersync for Voice is also supported through Alexa . It can track the current playback position of your audiobooks and pick up at the last bookmark.

Here are some commands relating to audiobooks:

Begin or continue listening to an audiobook that has been bookmarked >> "Read (title)" or "Play the book, (title)." or "Play the audiobook, (title)." or "Play (title) from Audible."

Pause Reading >> "Pause"

Resume listening to the most recent audiobook >> "Resume my book."

Go forward or backward by 30 seconds >> "Go back" or "Go forward"

Go to the previous or next chapter >> "Next chapter" or "Previous chapter"

Go to specific chapter >> "Go to chapter (#)"

Restart a chapter >> "Restart"

Reading Kindle Books on Echo Dot

You can ask Alexa to read Kindle books from your library. These include books that you have purchased from Kindle Store, borrowed from the Lending Library, borrowed from Kindle Unlimited and shared in your Family Library. When you ask Alexa to read your Kindle book, Alexa picks up from where you left off in the book.

<u>Some basic commands are-</u>

The Task	The Command
Listen to a Kindle book	"Read my Kindle book." "Read my book, '[title].'" "Play the Kindle book, '[title].'" "Read '[title].'"
Pause the Kindle book	"Pause." "Stop."
Continue listening to your Kindle book	"Play." "Resume."
Go to the next or previous paragraph	"Skip back." "Skip ahead." "Go back." "Go forward." "Next." "Previous."

NB: To go to different chapters in a Kindle book, select the **Now Playing** bar in the Alexa App when Alexa reads your Kindle book, and then select **Queue**. You can then choose a chapter from the list.

Managing Your To-Do List

Managing your to-do list is such a burden, isn't it? Alexa can help you with that. This will help you do the things you have to do such as attending an appointment without having a hard time!

Just say, "Alexa, add 'make juice' to my to-do list". The Echo Dot will add it automatically and update the list in your app accordingly.

You can also update the list manually from the app by going to the To-do list and adding an item.

Alexa can store up to 100 items per list. Everytime you remember something, you can tell Alexa to add in your to-do list. You can also delete some if you have to.

Some basic to-do list commands:

"Alexa, create a to-do list."

"Alexa, I need a vet's appointment."

"Alexa, I need to go to the Post Office on Monday."

"Alexa, put car wash to my to-do list."

Using Any Do and Todoist on Echo Dot

You can add third party list services like **_Any Do_** and **_Todoist_** with Echo Dot via Alexa. Here is how-

1. Open the left navigation panel on Alexa App.
2. Select **Settings** and then **Lists.**
3. Select **Link** for the list service.
4. Enter your login credentials for the third-party service.
5. Follow the on-screen prompts to complete the linking process.

Managing Timer with Echo Dot

Echo Dot can set a countdown timer. You can edit the timer any time with voice command or from the Alexa App after you have created a timer.

Some basic countdown timer commands are:

The Task	The Command
Set a countdown timer	"Set a timer for [amount of time]." "Set the timer for [time]."
Check time remaining on a countdown timer	"How much time is left on my timer?" (tells you how much time is left on your next upcoming timers)
Cancel or stop a countdown timer	"Stop the timer." (when timer is sounding). "Cancel the timer for [amount of time]." (for upcoming timers)

Managing Alarm with Echo Dot

Echo Dot can wake you up on your desired time. You can edit the alarm any time with voice command or from the Alexa App after you have created a new alarm.

Some basic countdown alarm commands are:

The Task	The Command
Set a single alarm	"Wake me up at [time]." "Set an alarm for [time]." "Set an alarm for [amount of time] from now."
Set a repeating alarm	"Set a repeating alarm for [day of week] at [time]." "Set an everyday alarm for [time]."
Snooze the alarm	"Snooze." (when alarm is sounding)
Check the status of your alarms	"What time is my alarm set for?" "What alarms do I have for [day]?" "What repeating alarms do I have?"
Cancel or stop an alarm	"Stop the alarm." (when alarm is sounding) "Cancel alarm for [time] on [day]." (turns off the alarm, but does not delete it)."

NB: Even if you mute Echo Dot, the alarm will still go off.

Deleting an Alarm

1. Select **Timers & Alarms** from the left navigation panel of **Alexa App**.

2. Choose your device from the drop-down menu.

3. Select the **Alarms** tab.

4. Select the alarm you want to delete, and then select **Delete** alarm.

Changing Alarm and Timer Volume

1. Select **Settings** from the left navigation panel of Alexa App.
2. Select your device.
3. Select **Sounds**.
4. Press and drag the volume bar for **Alarm and Timer Volume**.

Using Calendar on Echo Dot

You can link your Google Calendar account with Alexa. You can give command to add new events or recap upcoming events on your calendar.

Here is how you link your account to Alexa-

1. Open the Alexa App, go to the left navigation panel and tap on **Settings**.
2. Go to **Calendar** > **Google Calendar**.
3. Tap on **Link Google Calendar account**. When prompted, sign in with your Google email address and password.

Some basic commands are:

The Task	The Command
Find out about your next event	"When is my next event?" "What's on my calendar?"

Find out about an event at a specific time or on a specific day	"What's on my calendar tomorrow at [time]?" "What's on my calendar on [day]?"
Add an event to your calendar	"Add an event to my calendar." "Add [event] to my calendar for [day] at [time]."

Find Great Books and Restaurants

If you are looking for a romantic book, you can ask Alexa to search in the romance genre. Alexa will give you suitable options that you can choose from.

Alexa can give you a list of the best restaurants in your neighborhood. She can also give you the latest deals or promotions as far as restaurants are concerned. Just tell her, "Alexa, give me restaurant deals."

Flash Briefing, Live News, Traffic, Weather and Other Info

You need to add your address on Alexa App to make sure that these services work properly.

Adding or Changing Your Address

You need to add your address to Alexa App. This is how-

1. Open the left panel on the Alexa App and select **Settings**.
2. Select your Echo Dot device.
3. Go to Device **Location > Edit.**
4. Enter the complete address. Then tap on **Save.**

Listening to Flash Briefings

Alexa can deliver pre-recorded updates from popular broadcasters (from NPR, Economist, BBC News) through flash briefing services. The service also delivers the latest news headlines and weather updates.

In order to set up your **Flash Briefing** settings, follow these steps:

Step-1: In the Alexa app, open the left navigation panel and select **Settings > Flash Briefing**.

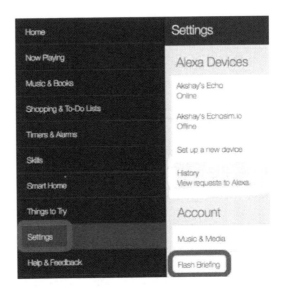

Step-2: Now you can customize the shows, news headlines and weather updates shown from different sources in your Flash Briefing screen with the on/off switches next to each part.

Commands to Alexa to Listen to Flash Briefings:

Listen to Flash Briefing >> "What's my Flash Briefing?" or "What's new?"

Navigate Through Flash Briefing or Cancel >> "Next", "Previous", "Cancel"

Listening to Weather Forecast

Alexa can provide you with the local weather forecast for updated conditions. Alexa can also provide you with the weather forecast for most US and international cities. Alexa receives the weather updates from AccuWeather.

To start off, you need to add a home address in the Alexa App.

When you ask about the weather update, a card will also appear in the Alexa app with a seven day forecast for the location requested.

Common commands for weather update:

Current weather in your location >> "What's the weather?"

Weather for a specific time period >> "What's the weather for this week?", "What's the weather for this weekend?", "What's the weather for (day)?"

Weather forecast in another city >> "What's the weather in (city, state)?", "What's the weather in (city, country)?"

Weather Conditions >> "Will it rain tomorrow?", "Will it be windy tomorrow?"

Listening to Sports Update

You can ask Alexa about the sports update, latest games and game fixture for upcoming games of your favorite sports teams.

First you need to go to Settings > Sports Update to set it up. You can add up to 15 sports teams.

Some Supported League are:

- National Football League (NFL)
- Major League Baseball (MLB)
- National Hockey League (NHL)
- National Basketball Association (NBA)
- English Premier League (EPL)
- Bundesliga (BL)
- NCAA Men's Basketball
- Women's National Basketball Association (WNBA)
- Major League Soccer (MLS)

How to add a sports team?

1. From the Alexa App, go to **Settings > Sports Update**.

2. Type the name of the team and select the team from the suggestions that appear. This will add the team to Sports Update.

3. To remove a team from the list, you can cross it out by selecting the **X** next to the team name.

Command to hear Sports Update:

Listen to sports update >> "Give me my Sports Update."

Checking Traffic News

Alexa can provide you information about the traffic conditions for your daily route, trip to the airport or a drive to the shopping mall. Specify a starting point and a destination point and Alexa will give you the traffic update, probable travel time and quickest route.

How to Set Up Daily Route Info?

1. From the Alexa app, go to **Settings > Traffic**.
2. Select **Change Address** in the "To" and "From" box.
3. Enter a starting point and destination address and select **Save changes**.
4. You also add up to one additional stop in a route by selecting **Add stop**.

Command to hear Sports Update:

Traffic Update >> "How is traffic?", "What's my commute?". "How's the traffic like right now?"

Finding Movie Showtime

Alexa can find movies playing in a nearby theatre or in another city. Alexa gets the information on movies and shows including cast, ratings and so on from IMDB.

You need to add your current location in the Alexa app.

Command to hear about movie showtime:

Which movies are playing >> "What movies are playing?"

Movies playing in another city >> "What movies are playing in (city)?"

Types of movies playing >> "What (genre) movies are playing?"

For a particular movie >> "When is (movie title) playing today?", "When will (movie title) play tomorrow?", "What movies are playing between (timeframe)?"

For information about a movie >> "Tell me about the movie (movie title)?"

Movies playing in a specific theatre >> "What movies are playing at (theatre name)?", "When is (movie title) playing (tomorrow/this weekend) at (theatre name)?"

Listening to Radio Programs

You can listen to your favorite radio stations on Echo Dot. You can listen to radio stations on Pandora, iHeartRadio and TuneIn.

Some basic commands are:

The Task	The Command
Play a custom station	"Play my (artist/genre) station on (Pandora/iHeartRadio/Prime Music)."
Play a Radio Station (TuneIn and iHeartRadio)	"Play (station frequency)" "Play the station (statin name)"
Play a podcast or program (TuneIn and iHeartRadio)	"Play the podcast (podcast name)" "Play the program (program name)"
Create a station (iHeartRadio and Pandora)	"Make a station for (artist name)." "Create an (iHeartRadio/Pandora) station based on (artist)"

Knowing Places Nearby on Echo Dot

You need to add your current location in the Alexa app.

Here are some basic commands:

The Task	The Command
Search for different types of businesses or restaurants nearby	"What [businesses / restaurants] are nearby?" "What [businesses / restaurants] are close by?"
Search for top-rated businesses or restaurants nearby	"What are some top-rated [businesses / restaurants]?"

Ask for the address of a nearby business or restaurant type	"Find the address for a nearby [business / restaurant]."
Ask for the phone number of a nearby business or restaurant type	"Find the phone number for a nearby [business / restaurant]."
Ask for the hours of a nearby business or restaurant type	"Find the hours for a nearby [business / restaurant]."
Ask about phone numbers, physical addresses, and business hours (after Alexa provides you with business information)	"What is the phone number?" "How far is it?" "Are they open?"

Getting Flight Information on Echo Dot

Alexa works with Kayak to help you track flight arrival and departure times. You can ask suitable flight arrival and departure times.

Basic commands:

The Task	The Command
Flight Arrival	"Alexa, ask Kayak when the flight from Boston will arrive,"
Tracking a flight	"Alexa, ask Kayak to track a flight, flight XXXXX "
Get fair or hotel suggestions	"Alexa, ask Kayak where I can go for $300," "Alexa, ask Kayak to search for hotels in Barcelona."

Using IFTTT with Echo Dot

IFTTT stands for "If This Then That". It is a third party service that helps you create rules. These rules (called the 'recipes') aid in automating the process of working together of apps and devices.

First, you have to activate the Amazon Alexa Channel on the IFTTT website. After that, you can use Echo Dot to execute recipes for different apps and websites, like Gmail, Twitter and Facebook.

You can also play around with alarms and timers.

In order to activate-

1. Go to the Amazon Alexa Channel on IFTTT and sign in. If you do not have an account, click on **Sign Up** to create one by following the on-screen instructions.
2. Once you have signed in, click on **Activate.**
3. Now sign in to your Amazon account so that you can link it to your IFTTT account.

Now you can select recipes that are available on Amazon Alexa Channel or you can create your own. Here is how:

1. Go to the Amazon Alexa Channel (https://ifttt.com/amazon_alexa) and sign in to your IFTTT account. Your IFTTT user name will appear in the top right corner of the website.
2. Click on your user name and then click on **Create** from the menu that pops up.
3. Where it says "ifthisthenthat" click on the word "this".
4. Find the Trigger Channel which is Amazon Alexa Channel and click on it to select it. If prompted, log in to your Amazon Alexa account.

5. Select an Amazon Echo Dot Trigger.

6. Click on **Create Trigger** and then click on the word "that" in "ifthisthenthat".

7. Choose an **Action Channel** – if you have not yet linked the selected channel to IFTTT, you have to do that first. Then click on **Activate Channel**.

8. Choose the action that Amazon Echo Dot is going to trigger.

9. Add in the data (called the "ingredients") to the recipe.

10. Choose **Create Action**

Alexa Skills

Alexa's skills can definitely help make life easier for you. If you know what needs to be done, you can utilize the skills properly.

How to Turn Alexa Skills on:

1. Open the Alexa app and tap on **Skills** from the left panel.

2. You see a list of all the skills. Tap on **Enable** for every Skill that you want to use.

3. If you don't want to use a skill, just click **Disable**.

NB: You can also enable skills from the Alexa Skills store on the website at https://www.amazon.com/skills

Here is a rundown of different skills of Alexa:

Skill Finder

There are around 1,900 skills of Alexa. Discovering new helpful skills can be a daunting task if you don't use the Skill Finder skill. It help you discover new skills. You can launch it by saying, "Alexa, open skill finder."

Finance Skills

Capital One

Capital One skill allows you to check your credit card balance or make a payment when a payment is due. It performs security checks with two layers of identity verification before letting you in. Be careful, however, of your surrounding because anyone who hears your personal codes may access your banking or credit card information just by asking Alexa.

Opening Bell

Opening Bell is a skill that allows you to ask for a stock price before heading out to work in the morning. For example, you can say, "Alexa, ask Opening Bell for the price of Apple."

Food Skills

Domino's

Ordering pizza has become a whole lot easier and lazier with the Domino's skill. You can place an order just by saying, "Alexa, open Domino's and place my Easy Order." If you want to track an order you have placed earlier, just say, "Alexa, open Domino's to track my order."

The Bartender

If you want to make a drink, but not sure of it's ingredients and the recipe, you can use The Bartender skill. You can ask Alexa what a drink is made of. Her response will help you dissect your favorite cocktails.

MySomm

MySomm skill can recommend a wine that pairs with a food. Just ask, "Alexa, ask Wine Gal what goes with Sizzling Salmon."

What beer?

"What beer?" is a similar skill that can suggest a matching beer for a dish. Just say, "Alexa, ask what beer what goes with pork chop."

Meat Thermometer

You can use Meat Thermometer skill to cross-check optimal cooking temperature for different meats. Say, "Alexa, ask Meat Thermometer what is the best temperature for beef steak."

Travel Skills

Kayak

Kayak skill can give you fare estimates for your upcoming tours. Just say, "Alexa, ask Kayak where can I go for $300" or "Alexa, ask Kayak how much it costs to fly from Louisiana to Colorado." This skill will ask you some additional question before providing you with some options and price ranges.

Uber

Alexa's integration with Uber can help you get a ride any time. Just say, "Alexa, ask Uber to get me a car."

Lyft

Lyft functions pretty much the same way, except you can ask for pricing. Say, "Alexa, ask Lyft how much a Lyft Plus from home to airport costs."

Productivity Skills

Quick Events

You can use Quick Events skill to add to your Amazon To-do list and transfer it to Google Calendar. Say, "Alexa, tell Quick Events to go to Church tomorrow at 8:00" You can also use

IFTTT to push your new additions to Amazon to-do list to Google Calendar. IFTTT integration will be discussed later on.

Giant Spoon

Giant Spoon skill can spill out some ideas for you that might be helpful if your job is marketing related or you are doing some sort of research of new things. Giant Spoon can definitely spark some interesting ideas for you.

Math Mania and 1-2-3 Math

These are two useful math skills if you want to brush up on your multiplication, addition, subtraction, or division capabilities.

To open, just say-

"Alexa, Open Math Mania".
"Alexa, Open 1-2-3".

Emails

You can email someone using Gmail by asking Alexa. Connect it to IFTTT and Alexa , and you are set to go!

Find Your Phone

Sometimes you lose your phone but you know it's around. When that happens, ask Alexa any sports score (for example, Alexa, what's the NFL score?) and Alexa will make your phone ring while answering your question.

Entertainment

The main entertainment skills include:

Angry Bard

You can ask the angry bard to say some insults and barbs if you want to hear some. The Angry Bard has a wide collection of insults from a wide range of literature including the work of Shakespeare.

Just say, "Alexa, ask Angry Bard for a burn" and Alexa will respond with something amusing.

Cat Facts

This gives some random funny cat facts. There are a couple of hundred of facts you can get, and each fact is unique.

Quote Me

Do you love to start your day by hearing an inspirational quote? Quote Me has over 75,000 quotes that cover over a hundred topics. These are quotes from famous people that range from Bill Gates, Sophocles, Walt Whitman among others.

If you feel down, you may ask your Alexa for a humor or happiness quote that will cheer you up. You can ask for a random quote or a quote on a specific topic.

Shower Thoughts

Shower Thoughts are itty-bitty witty bite-sized clever thoughts. This is a skill which will automatically fetch the Internet's most popular Shower Thought each day.

So do you want something to think about as you bathe? Ask Alexa to give you some shower thoughts.

Superpower

With Superpower, you can get an interesting conversation topic to start an engaging discussion with your friends and family. Exciting new topics are constantly being added to help you liven up your dinner parties and family gatherings.

Knock-Knock Jokes

If you love humor, this is for you. This skill gives funny and interesting knock-knock jokes.

Crystal Ball

It's a fortune telling skill. Alexa will ask you a few yes and no type of questions and then give an answer regarding what you want to know about.

Edgar Facts

This will give you all the facts about Edgar the Dog.

Music Quiz

You will get 100's of songs in a quiz format. Just say-

"Alexa, Launch Music Quiz."

Boo/Applause

You can boo or applause someone with realistic funny sound effects. To launch, just say-

"Alexa, ask Boo."
"Alexa, ask applause."

Fart

A hilarious skill for kids. Just say-

"Alexa, ask for a fart."

Games

The top game skills of Alexa include:

Trainer Tips

If you are a Pokémon Go fan and you want to get better at it, the Trainer Tips skill is for you. You can learn about various Pokemon that will help you do well in the game. Just say, "Alexa, ask Trainer Tips what's weak against water types." or "Alexa, ask Trainer Tips to give me a tip." or "Alexa, ask Trainer Tips to teach me something new."

If you have a lot of questions about Pokemon rather than one question, you can start by saying "Alexa, open Trainer Tips." Then you can do something like this:

YOU: "Alexa, open Trainer Tips."

ALEXA: "Welcome Trainer! I can help you choose the right team for battle. Ask me about a type's strengths or weaknesses, or ask for a trainer tip. "

YOU: "Alexa, what's weak against Steel?"

ALEXA: "Steel types are strong against ice, rock, and fairy type attacks. Steel types are also immune to Poison attacks."

YOU: "Alexa, What's strong against Rock?"

ALEXA: "Rock types are weak against water, grass, ground, fighting, and steel type attacks."

The Wayne Investigation

If you like mysteries and you are a Marvel geek, you will like The Wayne Investigation. This is an adventure game where you investigate the death of Bruce Wayne's parents. You will be presented with different prompts and need to make some choices. Each choice you make will affect the outcome of the story.

Typical commands to Alexa include-

"Alexa, open the Wayne Investigation."
"Chase thief."
"Visit crime lab."

Abra

Abra is another game that you might like. It is a character-guessing game. Guess a character and Abra will ask you questions and try to figure it out.

To play Abra, say "Alexa, start Akinator!" It is a great party game that can leave your guests wondering about the creepy accuracy of Alexa in figuring out the character.

The Magic Door

Another game that might interest you is The Magic Door. The Magic Door is an Alexa-powered interactive adventure game with original stories. You can tell Alexa about your choices as you go through a forest, a garden, or an ancient temple.

Just say, "Alexa, open the magic door" and get started. You can find hidden items, solve riddles, help magical creatures and find magical items to get a prize! Potions, dragons, fairies, gnomes, gods, and treasure await you as you explore the various places!

Animal Game

You think of an animal. Then just ask "Alexa, start the Animal Game." Alexa will ask you some yes or no type of questions in order to guess what animal it is.

Blackjack

You can ask Alexa to play the blackjack game for you.

Bingo

If you are a fan of Bingo game, you can play with the help of Alexa. Alexa can call the numbers for you while you play your bingo with cards.

Guess the Number

In this game, Alexa picks a number and you have to guess which number it is. With each guess, Alexa lets you know if it is higher or lower.

Tic-Tac-Toe and Hangman

Tic-tac-toe and hangman are easy games that your kids are sure to enjoy.

Just say-

"Alexa, Ask Hangman for a Game."

"Alexa, Ask Tic-Tac-Toe for a Game."

Smart Home & Car

Yonomi

Yonomi is a skill that is similar to IFTTT but designed exclusively for smart home. Yonomi is a native skill where you can ask Alexa to run any of your Routines that manage your favorite devices such as Sonos, Logitech Harmony and LIFX bulbs. The key phrase to say is: "Alexa, turn on [Routine Name]" You need to have an account with Yonomi and corresponding components of smart home installed in your home.

To set up Yonomi skill:

- Launch the Alexa App Tap on Menu > Smart Home > Yonomi
- Tap "Enable Skill" and sign into your Yonomi account

- Say "Alexa, discover devices" or tap "Discover devices" within the Smart Home tab of the Alexa app.

Automatic

Do you want Alexa to spill out some information on the status of your car? You can use the Automatic skill. The Automatic dongle can connect your smart phone with the OBDII port in your car. It can track the status of your car. Once you have connected your Automatic account to Alexa, you can ask Alexa where your car is, current fuel level or how far you have driven.

Lifestyle

The top lifestyle skills of Alexa include:

Campbell's Kitchen

You can ask Alexa to access Campbell's Kitchen to get you some quick dinner recipes and other relevant tips for preparing dinner.

Stub Hub

If you like to go away and party this weekend, Stub Hub skill will help you. With Stub Hub, Alexa can search for entertainment spots in your city or neighboring city and get you an update on what's going on and where.

Tide Pooler

If you live near the beach and want to know when the tide is high and when it is low, you can use this skill. Alexa can also tell you when it is the right time to go surfing.

You can get the comprehensive list of skills on the website at https://www.amazon.com/skills

Teaching Alexa More Skills

Of course, using Alexa doesn't just mean you're just going to take what's being offered and that you wouldn't be thinking of how it can be improved. If you really want to make Alexa yours, why not try the following tips below?

Help Alexa Compute

We're not talking about your basic $1 + 1 = ?$ Alexa can learn the concepts of floating decimals, so she can tell you the sum of 3.1416 and 2.24756 in a jiffy.

Allow Alexa to Research

While Alexa cannot recite the Prime Directive for you yet, she can tell you that it was also the title of a Star Trek movie. She can also access the Internet to give you direct facts and figures. She can even research how many calories that scoop of ice cream has!

Pop Culture Sense & Easter Eggs

Try asking Alexa to beam you up, or try asking her if she is Skynet, and she will give you hilarious answers.

She can respond to a wide variety of pop culture references, as well as a collection of **Easter eggs**. Keep on experimenting with commands.

Alexa,

- Do you want to fight?
- Do you want to build a snowman?
- Do you really want to hurt me?

- Do you like green eggs and ham?
- Do you know the way to San Jose?
- Do you know the muffin man?
- Do you know Siri?
- Do you have any brothers or sisters?
- Do you have a girlfriend?
- Do you love me?
- Where in the world in Carmen Sandiego?
- Where have all the flowers gone?
- What was the Lorax?
- What time is it in (name of city)?
- What is your quest?
- What is your favorite color?
- What is the sound of one hand clapping?
- What is the meaning of life?
- What is the loneliest number?
- What is the distance between (location a) and (location b)?
- What is the definition of_____?
- What is the best tablet?
- What is love?
- What does earth weight?
- What is the airspeed velocity of an unladen swallow?
- My milkshake brings all the boys to the yard.
- I am your father.
- Beam me up.
- Knock knock.
- Who are you wearing?
- Are you Skynet?
- Set phasers to kill.
- I shot a man in Reno.
- Up up down down left right left right b, a, start.

- I'm never gonna give you up.
- What's the first rule of Fight Club?
- Who are you going to vote for?
- Romeo, Romeo wherefore art thou Romeo?
- Is the tooth fairy real?
- Which comes first: The chicken or the egg?
- Hello HAL.
- Surely you can't be serious.
- Rock paper scissors.
- I want the truth.

Calculating Dates

Alexa has not yet learnt to check how many days there are before the next Superbowl, but you can ask her the number of days before Christmas arrives. You can even ask her how many days are left until your birthday (any date, as long as you specify it) and Alexa will respond accordingly.

Make Alexa Say What She Just Said Again

Just like when talking with other people, there may be times when you would not easily understand what Alexa has just said. What you can do then is ask Alexa to repeat her answer, and you can do this by saying "Alexa, can you repeat that?" Make sure you say this calmly, because saying "Repeat that" without "Please" or "Can You" just makes Alexa a bit more stubborn, as she wouldn't really repeat it.

Voice Training

Commands Get Better with Voice Training

Alexa is Echo Dot's AI, housed in a cloud server that allows her to grow and learn with each interaction. As her new master, however, you will be the one to show her the ropes --starting with understanding your speech.

The voice training session will accustom Alexa to your speaking patterns. You will be asked to speak 25 preset phrases. Before beginning, make sure that the Mic Off button has not been activated, and that you are in a location where you would normally be when you start regularly using the Echo Dot.

How to start voice training session?

To start the session, simply select "Voice Training" from the left panel of your Alexa app. If you made a mistake in speaking the phrase, simply hit Pause and the "Repeat Phrase" option. If you need to end the training for some reason, hit "End session" instead (also under Pause).

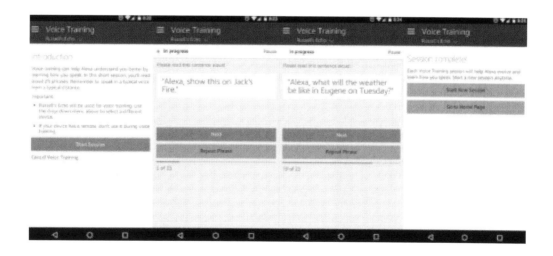

When you finish, click on "Go to Home Page"

Funny Conversations

Here are some funny conversations that you can have with Alexa:

- How many angels can dance on the head of a pin?
- How far is (location) from here?
- How do you make bread?
- How do I get rid of a dead body?
- High five!
- Good night.
- Give me a hug.
- Fire photon torpedoes.
- Elementary, my dear Watson.
- Does this unit have a soul?
- Do you want to play a game?
- Do you want to play a game?
- Do you believe in ghosts?
- Define supercalifragilisticexpialodocious.
- Count by ten.
- Can you give me some money? (ask twice)
- Beam me up.
- Are you sky net?
- Are you lying?
- Are you in love?
- Do you want to fight?
- Do you want to build a snowman?
- Do you really want to hurt me?
- How much is that doggie in the window?
- How much do you weigh?
- How many pickled peppers did Peter Piper pick?

- How many licks does it take to get to the center of a tootsie pop?
- How many calories are in (name of food)?

Creating a Smart Home

The Amazon Echo Dot device is capable of controlling compatible smart appliances within the household. This includes lights, switches, heaters, and many more. The Alexa app allows you to group all smart devices for easier and more efficient management.

For instance, you can group all smart lights in the kitchen in a single group. This way, you only need to assert the group name in your voice command instead of separating each device into multiple commands. The list of compatible smart products continues to grow.

This chapter will include the most common products used with the Amazon Echo Dot along with step by step installation process of some of them.

Philips Hue

Hue bulbs are one of the smartest products under the Philips brand. The brightness of these bulbs can be controlled and the light colors can be changed too.

Linking these devices to the Echo Dot speaker allows users to control the Philips Hue bulbs through voice commands. Make sure that all Hue bulbs were connected to the same Wi-Fi network.

Go to the Alexa app and search for the bulbs. Refer to the Philips user guide for how to connect the Philips Hue to the Wi-Fi network.

Steps to Control Philips Hue Lights with Echo Devices

1. From the Alexa app, go to Menu icon > Smart Home.
2. Under the Devices section, select Discover Devices.
3. Press the button on the Philips Hue Bridge. Now your Philips Hue devices should appear in the Devices section of Alexa app.
4. You can tap on each of these devices and assign names to them.
5. It is always better to create a group of lights so that you can control more than one light with a single command. To create a group, go to Settings > Groups > Create a Group. For example, you can create a group named "Living Room" to control all the lights in your living room.

Controlling Philips Hue Lights via IFTTT

You need to have your Philips Hue lights and Alexa apps set up first. You will also need an IFTTT account. Create an IFTTT account from www.ifttt.com .

1. First, you need to authorize Alexa to work with your IFTTT account. Visit www.ifttt.com and sign in.
2. From Channels home page, click Amazon Alexa.
3. Enter your login credentials of Amazon account. This will authorize Alexa to work with IFTTT.
4. Open the IFTTT app and tap Create an Applet.
5. Tap This button of "ifthisthenthat". Here you will need to select a trigger.

6. Select the Amazon Alexa icon.

7. Tap on "Say a specific phrase".

8. Type the phrase you wish to use. For example, if you wish to change the light color of Philips Hue light to red, just type "lights to red" and tap Next.

9. Tap That.

10. Tap the Philips Hue icon.

11. Tap Change Color. Here you can add the color you would like to change to and the lights which you want to change color. Then tap Next.

12. Press Finish. This will activate the applet.

It is all set! All you have to do is give the command, "Alexa, trigger lights to red." Alexa will comply.

After successfully pairing the bulbs with the Echo, you can now manage the lights with these commands:

"Alexa, dim the lights to 50 percent."
"Alexa, turn off the lights."

If you grouped the lights, then you use the following format for your voice command:

"Alexa, switch on [group name]."

Lutron

Lutron lights not only give you light, they are dimmable, too. Lutron Dimmers are simple to install, easy to work with and relatively cheaper.

Setting up Lutron Dimmers Step by Step

1. Make sure that you have all the switches and Lutron dimmers installed in proper locations.
2. Install the free Lutron app in your smartphone.
3. You need to install the Caseta wireless system and the Lutron Caseta wireless bridge by following the step by step guideline outlined the website: www.lutron.com
4. Pair your Amazon account with the Alexa enabled Echo device.
5. From the Alexa app, go to Menu > Smart Home.
6. Go to Device Links > Lutron > Link with Lutron.
7. Sign in with your Lutron smart bridge username and password.
8. After the sign in is complete, you should see a message, "Alexa has successfully linked with Lutron."
9. Go back to the Smart Home screen and go to Devices and tap Discover devices. You can also give command, "Alexa, discover my devices."
10. It will take a minute to discover your Lutron lights.
11. Now you can control the individual lights with voice commands.

Creating a Group of Lutron Lights

If you wish to control more than one light or all lights with a simple command, you have to create groups in the Alexa app. Here is how-

1. Under Devices, go to Groups > Create group.
2. Name your group.
3. Add the Lutron Caseta wireless lights that you wish to add and click save.

You can now manage the lights with these commands:

- "Alexa, turn my [group name] lights off."
- "Alexa, turn my living room lights on."
- "Alexa, turn off my table lamp."

LIFX Wi-Fi Smart Bulb

The LIFX LED Smart Bulb is a Wi-Fi enabled, energy efficient, multi-coloured lightbulb that you can control on your smartphone, tablet and with voice commands via Alexa. Suitable for home or professional use, the LIFX Smart Lightbulb puts a wide array of lighting colors at your fingertips.

With a wide variety of colors to choose from, the LIFX LED Smart Lightbulb allows you to set the mood, whatever it may be. The LIFX LED Smart Lightbulb can be programmed to wake you up each morning with a gradual increase in brightness and to help you drift off at night by steadily dimming the light. As well as giving you excellent control over the lighting in your home, the LIFX LED Smart Lightbulb can also be used to create the perfect ambience in retail, hospitality and commercial environments.

Setting up and Controlling LIFX Bulbs Step by Step

1. Download and install the LIFX app from Apple store or Google Play store.
2. Open the LIFX app. Go to Integrations and tap on Amazon Echo button.
3. From the page that pops up, login to your Amazon account. Tap on Authorize. This will give Echo the access to your LIFX bulbs.
4. Open the Alexa app. Go to Settings > Connected Home.
5. Tap Discover devices. This will discover the LIFX bulbs that are connected to the same wireless network.
6. You can tap on each of these devices and assign names to them. Now you can control these devices with their specific names with simple voice commands to Alexa.
7. It is always better to create a group of lights so that you can control more than one light with a single command. To create a group, go to Settings > Groups > Create a Group. For example, you can create a group named "Living Room" to control all the lights in your living room.

Controlling LIFX Lights via IFTTT

You will need an IFTTT account. Create an IFTTT account from www.ifttt.com .

1. First, you need to authorize Alexa to work with your IFTTT account. Visit www.ifttt.com and sign in.
2. From Channels home page, click Amazon Alexa.
3. Enter your login credentials of Amazon account. This will authorize Alexa to work with IFTTT.
4. Open the IFTTT app and tap Create an Applet.
5. Tap This button of "ifthisthenthat" . Here you will need to select a trigger.
6. Select the Amazon Alexa icon.
7. Tap on "Say a specific phrase".
8. Type the phrase you wish to use. For example, if you wish to change the light color of LIFX light to blue, just type "lights to blue" and tap Next.

9. Tap That.

10. Tap the LIFX icon.

11. Tap Change Color. Here you can add the color you would like to change to and the lights which you want to change color. Then tap Next.

12. Similarly, you can change the brightness and transition duration.

13. Press Finish. This will activate the applet.

It is all set! All you have to do is give the command, "Alexa, trigger lights to blue." Alexa will comply.

You can now manage your LIFX lights with these commands:

- Alexa, Turn the lights on.
- Alexa, Turn the Kitchen light off.
- Alexa, dim Bedroom lights by 25%.
- Alexa, turn on Movie Night Scene.
- Alexa, Switch lights to 50% brightness.
- Alexa, lower brightness by 25%.
- Alexa, activate My Pink Scene.

Nest Thermostat

Nest Thermostat is a smart thermostat that learns about your preferences and makes automatic changes so that you don't have to touch it. You can control it with voice command by adding it to Amazon Echo.

You need a Nest account and have your Nest Thermostat set up before integrating it with Alexa.

Setting up and Controlling Nest Thermostat Step by Step

1. Open the Alexa app on your phone.
2. Go to Menu icon > Smart Home.
3. Scroll down to find Get More Smart Home Skills and tap on the arrow.
4. Type "Nest" in the search box and tap the Nest logo from search results.
5. Tap Enable Skill.
6. Log in to your Nest account.
7. Select Accept.
8. From Alexa app, go to Devices and tap Discover devices. Within one minute, your Nest Thermostat should appear in your search result.
9. Tap on the Nest device and rename it. For example, if the thermostat is located in your dining room, you can name it "Dining Room"
10. Of course, you can create a group of thermostats and control those with a single voice command.

You can now manage Nest Thermostat with these commands:

* Set a specific temperature: "Alexa, set (thermostat name) to 70", " Alexa, change the Baby Room to 66 degrees."

- Incrementally raise and lower temperature: "Alexa, lower the (thermostat name) by 4 degrees"
- Give 2 degree increase or decrease commands: "Alexa, cool down (thermostat name)", "Alexa, turn the temperature up.", "Alexa, turn the temperature down."

Ecobee3 Thermostat

Ecobee3 is a smart thermostat that learns about your preferences and makes automatic changes.

Just like Nest, you can control it with voice command by adding it to Amazon Echo devices.

Setting Up and Controlling Ecobee3 Thermostat Step by Step

1. Open the Alexa app on your phone.
2. Go to Menu icon > Smart Home.
3. Scroll down to find Get More Smart Home Skills and tap on the arrow.
4. Type "Ecobee" in the search box and tap the Ecobee logo from search results.
5. Tap Enable.
6. When prompted, provide the Login information to link the accounts..
7. Under the authorize app screen, select Accept. Now you will see a message "Alexa has been successfully linked with ecobee."

8. From Alexa app, go to Devices and tap Discover devices. Within one minute, your Ecobee Thermostat should appear in your search result.

9. Tap on the Ecobee device and rename it. For example, if the thermostat is located in your dining room, you can name it "Dining Room"

10. Of course, you can create a group of thermostats and control those with a single voice command.

You can manage Ecobee3 thermostat with following voice commands:

- Set to a specific temperature: "Alexa, set living room temperature to 67."
- Raise or lower the temperature: "Alexa, raise the hallway temperature by 3 degrees."
- Increase or decrease the temperature by 2 degrees: "Alexa, heat up my bedroom.", "Alexa, increase the hallway temperature", "Alexa, lower the bedroom temperature", "Alexa, decrease the dining room temperature ", "Alexa, cool down the baby room."

Belkin WeMo

Users of WeMo devices can also pair them with the Amazon Echo .The speaker will automatically detect the WeMo device if connected to the same Wi-Fi network.

As of today, the only WeMo devices compatible with the Amazon Echo are the following:

- WeMo Switch
- WeMo Light Switch
- WeMo Insight

Setting up WeMo Switches Step by Step

1. Download the WeMo app from the App store or Google Play store.
2. Connect your WeMo switch to your Wi-Fi network.
3. Select the WeMo switch from the app and tap Edit. Now rename your switch. For example, you can name it "TV" so that when you say "Alexa, turn on the TV", Alexa can comply. Tap Save.
4. From the WeMo app, tap More > Remote Access > Enable Remote Access.
5. Open the Alexa app and tap Menu icon > Smart Home.
6. Go to Your Devices and tap Discover devices. Within one minute, your WeMo Smart Switch should appear under your devices.

Typical Voice Commands to Control WeMo Smart Switch:

- "Alexa, turn on switch name."
- "Alexa, turn off switch name."
- "Alexa, turn off the lamp."

SmartThings

Smart products under the SmartThings label are also compatible with the Echo Dot device. This ranges from lights, power outlets, and switches.

The SmartThings power outlets allow you to control any device or appliances that were plugged in. This means that you can also control non-smart appliances using the Amazon Echo Dot via SmartThings power outlets.

Link the SmartThings device to the Amazon Echo through the Alexa app.

Go to Settings and look for "Connected Home". You will be able to link the smart devices from there. The voice commands that you can do is similar to the Philips Hue voice commands.

Wink

Wink hub, similar to SmartThings power outlets, functions as a central device to help you manage Wink-compatible devices.

Here is the list of devices that are currently compatible with both Wink hub and Amazon Echo Dot:

Commercial Electric

- Smart LED Downlight

Cree

- Connected LED Bulb

EcoSmart

- Smart A19
- Smart PAR20
- Smart GU10
- Smart BR30

<u>GE</u>

- Link A19
- Link BR30
- Link PAR38

<u>Leviton</u>

- Z-wave Scene Capable Dimmer
- Z-wave Scene Capable Switch
- Z-wave Scene Capable Receptacle

Some items of the following brands:

- Lutron
- Osram
- Phillips
- TCP

Insteon

Aside from SmartThings and Wink, Amazon Echo Dot is also compatible with Insteon hub. You can also control all the devices plugged in the Insteon hub. As of the writing of this book, the only compatible Insteon hub so far is the Hub 2245 – 222.

Pairing this hub to the Alexa app will allow you to use the Echo Dot device in triggering connected appliances and lights.

August Smart Lock

You can enhance the security of your home by simple voice commands such as "Lock the front door." Thus, you can basically give the keys of your kingdom to Alexa.

With the August skill, you can ask Alexa to control your August Smart Locks. However, you have to use the extra language "tell August" when commanding your Alexa (for example, "Alexa, tell August to lock the front door."

August locks are compatible with majority of the standard deadbolts. It also gives you virtual keys for your family or friend. In addition, it can restrict access during specific times of the day. As of now, you cannot open the lock with voice commands.

You will need the August lock already installed, the August app and an August account before starting the integration with Alexa.

Setting up and Controlling August Smart Lock Step by Step

1. Open the Alexa app from your smartphone and go to Menu > Skills.
2. Search for the August skill and tap "August Home" from search results.

3. Tap Enable to activate the skill.

4. Enter your August email address and password in order to link your August account with Alexa.

5. You need to enter the code (that will be sent to your cell phone) in the blank box. Tap Verify.

6. In the next screen, tap Agree.

7. At this point, the August lock is ready to be controlled by your voice command via Alexa.

Typical Voice Commands to Control August Home lock:

- "Alexa, tell August to lock my door."
- "Alexa, ask August to lock my front door."
- "Alexa, tell August to test the state of the lock"

Other Smart Home Devices

Here are some other useful ways you can control gadgets and equipment in your home:

- Lutron dimmers to control dimmable lights.
- Garageio Door Control and Garageio skill to control your garage door.
- Nest Cam Outdoor and Indoor Security Camera.
- Haiku Home L-series Ceiling Fans.
- TP Link Smart Plugs and Switches.
- Neato Botvac Wi-Fi Vacuum Cleaners.

Some Other Useful Stuffs

Adding a Voice Remote on Echo Dot

If you tend to sit too far away from your Echo Dot speaker to efficiently control it, such as from the kitchen while the speaker lives in the living room, you might need a Voice Remote Control for Echo Dot.

Pair the remote in the **Settings** menu in the Alexa app, and you can remotely talk to your Echo from across the house, in other rooms or even while outside.

Deleting Voice Data History on Echo Dot

There are two ways to delete voice data history from Alexa:

1: Delete individual recordings

From the Alexa App, go to **Settings > History**. You'll see a list of all the requests you've made since setting up your Echo. To delete a recording, tap it, then tap **Delete voice recordings**.

2: Delete everything

For those who don't take chances, there's a way to delete all voice data at one go. Head to www.amazon.com/myx, sign in, and click **Your Devices**. Select **Amazon Echo Dot**, then click **Manage Voice Recordings**.

Sending Flowers to Someone via Echo Dot

To send flowers, you need to have an account with the flower and gift e-retailer **1-800-Flowers**. Also, you need to have the payment information added and the addresses of the corresponding persons linked with your account.

Just enable the **1-800-Flowers skill** from the Alexa app. Then sign in to your 1-800-Flowers account. This will integrate your 1-800-Flowers account with your Echo device.

Typical commands for Alexa are:

"Alexa, ask 1-800-Flowers to order Tulip flowers."

"Alexa, tell 1-800-Flowers I want to send flowers to Joanna on March 23rd."

"Alexa, tell 1-800-Flowers I need a large Love and Romance arrangement for Paul."

The flowers will be delivered to your contact's address in your 1-800-Flowers account. Your existing payment credentials in your 1-800-Flowers account will be used to pay for the delivery, so there is no need to enter additional payment information. It has never been easier to show those you love that you care.

Controlling Plex Media Center with Amazon Echo Dot

Do you happen to use the media streaming app Plex and also have an Amazon Echo device? Plex has already announced support for the Amazon Alexa voice assistant and the platforms it supports. The integration lets you control your movie, music, and TV show collections with your voice — and put away all the remotes cluttering up your living room table.

To set it up, tell Alexa to enable the **Plex skill**. From there, just link your account and ask Alexa to "Open Plex" to start using the skill.

Once you get it set up, you can say things like "Alexa, ask Plex what's new?" for a list of titles recently added to your Plex library. When you're ready to watch or listen to something, just say "Alexa, ask Plex to play…" followed by whatever it is you're in the mood for. Alexa and Plex can understand really specific requests, such as "…play season 3, episode 2 of The Goldbergs."

Plex has also integrated suggestions within its Alexa skill. You can, for instance, say "Alexa, ask Plex to suggest some music to listen to" or "Alexa, ask Plex to get this party started."

Adding Non-supported Smart Home Devices with Alexa

If you've got a mixture of smart home devices, chances are, there may be a few that aren't officially supported by Alexa. But there is a work around.

First, double-check that there isn't an Alexa Skill for that smart device. It there isn't, check the online connection sites Yonomi (https://yonomi.co) and IFTTT (www.ifttt.com) to see if your devices are supported.

If so, get to know Yonomi or IFTTT, as they can greatly expand the usefulness of Alexa, allowing you to tie several actions to a single voice command, export your Alexa to-do or shopping list to Apple Reminders or Todoist and much more.

Managing Your Car with Alexa

Automatic Skill is an extremely useful car-related skill. For this skill to synchronize with your car, you need to have the **Automatic Car Adapter** and connect that to your on-board diagnostic port. This device can pair with your smartphone via Bluetooth.

The **Automatic Car Adapter** device lets you monitor the gas mileage, car's GPS location and diagnose potential maintenance issues. You can sync this device with your Echo device.

Thus, with simple voice commands, you can know where you parked your car the last time, how much gas is left, how many miles you drove last month and so on. Some car related commands of Automatic for Alexa are:

- "Alexa, ask Automatic where's my car?"
- "Alexa, ask Automatic what's my fuel level?"

- "Alexa, ask Automatic how many miles I drove last month?"

Adding Family Members to Echo Dot

You and any of your family members can use the same Echo device simultaneously. All you have to do is download the Alexa app in both the phones and sync with Echo device.

How to add a household member to Amazon Echo Device:

- Add a household member to your Amazon Echo.
- Open the Amazon Alexa application or go to echo.amazon.com in a browser from your computer and navigate to Settings.
- Scroll to the bottom of Settings and locate Household Profile. Enter your Amazon log-in info and sign in.
- On the next page, click Continue.
- Next, give the computer or phone to the person you are adding to the account so he or she can enter the log-in information for that Amazon account.
- Once that's done, click Join Household.

With multiple accounts, not only can you share your content libraries, such as books and music; you can also collaborate on stuff like shopping lists, to-do lists and calendars.

To access the digital content from another user's account, you will need to switch to that person's profile by saying, "Alexa, switch accounts" or "Alexa, switch to Taylor's profile." To check which profile is currently active, simply ask, "Alexa, which account is this?" or "Alexa, which profile am I using?"

How to remove a household member:

- Open the Amazon Alexa app on your smartphone or navigate to **echo.amazon.com** from your browser from a computer and go to **Settings**.

- Near the bottom of Settings, you should see a menu titled **In an Amazon household with [user name]**. Select this.
- Beside your name, you should see a button titled Leave.
- Beside the other users' names, you will see the option to remove the user.
- Tap this link to remove a user or tap Leave to remove yourself from the household.

Troubleshooting

How to reset Echo Dot?

If for some reason, your Echo Dot is not responsive or isn't working the way it should be, you can reset the device. Here is how to reset your Echo Dot :

1. Press the **Microphone off** and **Volume down** button together and hold for about 20 seconds until the light ring turns orange. Then the light will turn blue.

2. The light ring will now turn off and then it will turn on again. Then the light ring will turn orange again. At this point the Echo Dot will enter the set up mode.

3. Open the Alexa app from your smart phone or computer, connect to a Wi-Fi network and register it to your Amazon account, just like you did the first time. You device is reset now.

Echo Dot Not Connecting to Wi-Fi

First, restart the Echo Dot. Just unplug the adapter from the power source and plug it in again.

If it still doesn't connect, you need to reset Echo Dot.

- Press and hold the **Microphone Off** and **Volume Down** button together for around 20 seconds until the light rings turns orange.

- Then the light ring will turn blue. Then the light ring go off and come up again. Now the light ring will turn orange.

- Your Echo Dot will enter setup mode. You need to open the Alexa App , connect the Echo Dot to your Wi-Fi network and register it with your Amazon credentials.

Echo Dot Does Not Respond

- Make sure you use the included 9W power adapter. Other adapters (like cell phone chargers) do not provide enough power for Echo Dot to turn on and work correctly.
- Press the **Action** button for five seconds to see if Echo Dot responds to your requests.
- When you connect your Echo Dot to a speaker (through Bluetooth or the audio cable), make sure your Echo Dot is at least three feet away from the speaker.
- Make sure your device is at least eight inches away from walls or other objects.
- Make sure there is no background noise when you speak.

Device Misunderstands You

Make sure that there are no loud background noises when you issue commands to the speaker device. You might also try speaking slowly and clearly. Don't forget to finish the voice training session as well to help the device in recognizing how you speak better.

Lost Confirmation Code

Go to the Alexa app and select "Settings" on the navigational panel. Look for "Voice Purchasing" and you can set a new confirmation code from there. Remember to use the new code when making purchases via voice command.

Echo Dot Not Connecting to an External Speaker via Bluetooth

- Try to connect your smartphone to the speaker. If it connects, your bluetooth speaker is ok.
- Make sure to unpair other devices from the speaker.
- For portable speakers, check the batteries for the speaker.
- Check for interference. Move your Bluetooth speaker and Echo Dot away from microwave ovens, baby monitors, and other wireless devices.
- In the Alexa app, forget the Bluetooth speaker. Go to **Settings** > **Echo Dot** > **Bluetooth** in the app, and then select your Bluetooth speaker. Select **Forget Device** to unpair the speaker from Echo Dot.
- Try to reconnect to the Bluetooth speaker to Echo Dot. Set the speaker to pairing mode, and then say, "Pair."

For more troubleshooting of your Alexa device, please visit the following link:
https://www.ifixit.com/Wiki/Amazon_Echo_Troubleshooting

Do's and Don'ts for Amazon Echo Dot

With a new kind of technology, like the Echo Devices, it is a general consequence that thieves, hackers, spammers and scammers will try to utilize any opportunistic loopholes. You need to make sure that your Echo device stays safe from some unintended consequences.

If you have smart home facilities and control appliances integrated with Echo Dot:

- Don't position your Echo device near a window.
- Don't position it near a speakerphone answering machine.
- When you will be away from home, push the mute button to avoid unwanted usage or wake ups.

I also suggest you get a Protection Plan (2 years plan is the most used) for your Echo device. Most of the reported failures of Echo devices have occurred because of accidents (such as dropping off a table, dropping in water, dog chewing etc.) . The protecting plan will have your Echo device covered against accidental damage.

Video Tutorials

To see some useful **video tutorials** on Amazon Echo Dot, please visit the following page from your web browser:

http://www.homezenith.com/echo-dot-videos/

Bonus Ebook

As a gratitude to you for purchasing this guide, I have a special bonus for you. It is the-

199 Funny Things You Can Ask Alexa

Please visit **www.homezenith.com/alexa** to claim it today for free!

Conclusion

The Echo Dot 2nd generation comes with just about everything the users need from an intelligent Alexa device. Thank you for getting this Echo Dot guide. I hope you have enjoyed it as much as I did while preparing it. If you have any query, please send me an email at info@homezenith.com.

I would request for your honest feedback on this guide.

Please Leave Your Review on the Amazon Page
Where You Ordered this Guide

Meanwhile, please visit my website **www.homezenith.com** for all the latest stylish modern interior design ideas for your home.

Have fun!

Ray Higgins

Printed in Germany
by Amazon Distribution
GmbH, Leipzig